THE ISLAND

THE ISLAND

ERIN GEARY

Copyright © 2021 by Erin Geary

All rights reserved. No part of this book may be reproduced in any manner whatsoever without written permission except in the case of brief quotations embodied in critical articles and reviews.

First Printing, 2021

Contents

Dedication   vi

1. People and Their Environment   1
2. Grey   10
3. Angels   19
4. Solar Eclipse   31
5. Sandwiches   42

For Grandpa

I

People and Their Environment

I feel safe in the first subway car. There's a window that faces into the tunnel, just over the shoulder of the train operator. I like to hover my nose next to it, my breath fogging the glass. The New York City subway system is so black on the inside that it becomes colorful again. It reminds me of what happens when you close your eyes and press down on your lids: a mirage of greens and purples, a slippage between this world and heaven.

I pretend to drive the train. When we approach a stop, I get to see people freckling the platform ahead. They hardly look like humans. At first, they are just tiny dots. As we pull closer, they morph into noses and fingers, suit jackets and wool coats, headphones and *Knicks* hats. I am weightless as I breeze past the crowd. They elbow each other in desperation, almost losing limbs in the train's closing doors.

Nobody ever has the patience to walk up to the first car. I

am often alone up here. Once, there was a woman with many suitcases—bags and bags and bags. Still, she seemed to make room for me, as if I were the one carrying too much.

I arrive on campus at the same time as this guy Terrence from 10 AM Geography class, *People and Their Environment*, a prerequisite Hunter College asks its freshmen to fill. He fishes for his ID card, loose in his back jeans pocket, and we wait to swipe into the building. He scats his fingers on his thigh, purring the lyrics to "Superstition" under his breath.

"Stevie Wonder," I say. "Great song." It's a nervous, innocuous burst of small-talk.

"Yeah. My parents raised me on him. A Detroit brother too."

"You're from Detroit?"

"What's left of it. They're gentrifying us real bad." This feels like its been at the edge of his lips all morning. "All the stress is wringing my Pop's neck." It's the first time I imagine whiteness like that: something with hands large enough to coil around a grown man's body like a snake.

The elevator up is broken, so I watch the bounce of his backpack near my nose as we climb the crowded staircase, its walls a silent grey, to the 6th-floor lecture hall. "Detroit," he says, wistful, licking his teeth at the T, humming, "*Mmmmm-michigan.*" He sings his city.

We slide into seats side-by-side as our professor sizes her PowerPoint presentation on the projector. Terrence gently describes a buried Detroit. I feel emotional and tiny, how I used to feel when my mom would sing lullabies to me. Each memory he finds is a snowflake. My favorite is one about the shoddy jazz club where his piano teacher let him try his first sip of beer. "It was around the corner from the Motown Museum, like its kid sister." Detroit sounds like a step touch, the sneer of a sax, home.

Terrence and I are almost friends, but never all the way. I've been having trouble making friendships stick here. They melt fast. They feel shapeless, intangible. This is probably my fault, but I find myself blaming the city, like New York is an overgrown jungle where weeds and branches clutter all its paths.

The problem is: I don't know how to fit, yet, into a world that knows me, a world in which I've escaped the comfort of being ignorant to myself. I am colorful and defined, but aware of how I bruise a room. I don't understand why every coming-of-age movie is about figuring out who you are. It's much harder to wear the empty nest of your body—it betrayed by the ways you've up and gone and changed.

* * *

Every day, it looks uglier outside. There's always a wet newspaper injured under the turnstile, a garbage bag slouching on the curb. The world sure knows how to ambush. I fill up my MetroCard in small bursts, unable to commit to the unlimited pass.

I follow these New York art students on Instagram who post with the casual intimacy of friends. They write about intersectional feminism and police abolition and socialism. Every day, I learn a new word for an old thing. I link into a history of people wanting better.

They all get photographs of their auras taken at this jewelry shop on Canal Street, the buzzy strip parting vibrant Chinatown and minimalistic SoHo like a wall.

So, I go. I want to run into those girls beneath the drip of the neon signage. Maybe one of them will take me back to their dorm, and we can fall asleep in a bed together like twins in the womb.

There's a woman at the jewelry shop who explains your photo to you afterward in something between a psychic reading and a therapy appointment. In my photo, I'm inside a dungeon of red. "Your stress is loud," she winces. Her hand covers the Polaroid as if to stop it from blinding her. "No menstruation?" she frowns, rubbing her abdomen. I feel see-through. She's right: I stopped bleeding a few months ago, when I began school, my body tricked by its sudden isolation, how the air smells different here.

The woman's eyes widen. She calls over another shop employee who, gasping, reaches a single finger to prod my chest. It's the first time I've been touched all day. "Special. Rare," she tells me, my body glitching from the invasion. On the aura photograph, my heart is haloed in a faint pink circle.

Presence and absence intersect in me. The women let me leave without paying, saying my aura brought "good luck."

I get catcalled coming out of the shop. The man is tall and spits on the street. I keep my jaw hard and walk fast, pulling my fists out of my coat pockets, my knuckles cold and bluing. He goes, "You women these days have such *ugly* hearts," but I have a pink halo, and I am not scared.

***

I have a poetry professor named Paul. He brings pots and pans into class and we bang on them, like drums, to the rhythm of our pieces until we get noise complaints.

Mid-semester, his wife dies. The death is unexpected—apparently—and within hours, we receive a sterile, thin e-mail, saying, "Don't worry. Tomorrow's class is still on." When he shows up, his necktie is loose and confused. I wonder if she used to tie it for him, or if his hands stopped working last night, or if he had to loosen it just to breathe.

As Paul sits, his chair whimpers. It's Oliver's assigned day to workshop. When Paul doesn't speak, just stares into the lives of us, Oliver begins distributing photocopies of his poem, a sonnet about having bad sex with a single mom he dog-sits for. It's curt and inappropriate, like smoking over a hospital bed. "Aw, shit," he mutters, before placing one in front of Paul, face down on the desk.

A siren shrieks on the street. Usually, Paul's class is the only one that drowns out Manhattan. Today, it's here, just beyond the window. He says, "When you're sad, you're able to see the sadness of others so much more clearly. There's no fuzz."

I expect to find defeat in his face, but, instead, he trembles, like he's come face-to-face with God, awed and submissive. His forehead is flushed and veiny. I wonder what it might mean that he came here—of all places—in the aftermath of his wife's passing. Surely, he had somewhere to go, didn't he?

"Oliver, I'm pushing you to next week. I need to get my color back," he decides, hastily collecting the photocopies. We leave the classroom and walk together to Bethesda Terrace in Central Park, Paul leading the twelve of us. The tall Upper East Side buildings cut shadows in the sun on his bald head. It's strangely warm for December, like the world is ending.

He lets us wander, but I stay fastened to him, troubled by his energy. I've seen this place in movies. Street performers tinsel the fountain, lean against the arches and pillars, lounge into the hip of a cello on the stairs. There's a sculpture of an angel atop the fountain, and she rains water down on three twirling cherubs, her toe pointed like a dancer's.

Paul and I stop to watch one particular musician, a violinist with hair collected in a careful ponytail at the nape of her neck. Her bow sobs on the instrument's strings. The music seems to witness me—it and I both hollow and complicated at the same time. A tear cliffs off my eyelid, stubborn like a hangnail. I catch it in my mouth, and it tastes like me: the palatial ballroom of my brain, my cleanest parts.

As if I allowed him to, Paul cries, as well. His tears come out like wads of hair from a clogged shower drain. He coughs. We water our gardens. There is home at the Bethesda Terrace, growing up, bullheaded, like weeds through concrete.

I want to tell him that a glass filled to the brim is abundant, not precarious. I want to tell myself that everything can be seen in two ways. Instead, the violin tells us, *"You're here. You're here. You're here,"* and maybe that's all we needed: to hear that. Together.

***

On campus, noise curdles in the air. It raises high into the ceiling and stays there: years, decades of noise, thick, clunky build-up. The school preserves the noise and calls it "history." The school doesn't flush anything clean, the way my suburban high school would, each summer rinsing and scrubbing.

It overwhelms me, at first, to have to hear the world, as if hearing the world would mean deafening what I know of myself. Then, I wonder if all that sound could help me piece together my own voice, the way an artist would make a collage.

***

I worry about the final exam for *People and Their Environment* but pass with an A. Terrence tells me he passed, too, on our way out of the West Building into day-old snow. "I just hope the credit transfers," he admits, stopping to wipe the soggy toe of his sneaker.

"What? Why?" We hover at a crosswalk.

"I'm going back home. My family gets *weird* about me being here, like I'm leaving them behind or something." He puts a string from his hoodie in his mouth and chews on it. "There's a state school that's fine for now. They want me to work at my mom's hair salon—cleaning, sweeping, that sort of thing. They can't afford to pay another kid to do it." We walk a few blocks in silence, processing things, then he points at a Thai place. "I'm meeting someone for lunch." I try to decide if I'm upset. Something about the whole conversation feels like having a nightmare about having a nightmare, like I don't have the grounds to feel anything at all.

I nod. "Are you sad you're leaving?"

"No. New York won't miss me. There are *so many* of me here."

***

At our end-of-semester reading, Paul announces he's retiring, moving somewhere his grief can live, too. On a small stage in the Theater Building, he admits into the microphone, "I'm trying to fit a lot in my apartment right now. I just don't have enough room."

I think death is a lot like the inside of the subway tunnel. Death is the color you'd see swirling in a mood ring. It's dark, but not empty. It's dark, but not bare.

We tend to evaluate darkness by taking stock of what it's missing, but what does it hold? What does it home?

I wish I had Terrance's phone number, but I don't.

***

On my last day before Winter Break, I go into Dylan's Candy Bar, around the corner from my school. I fall for the screaming colors of its storefront the way one would fall for a third or fourth drink at the bar. It's bustling with tourist children, running wildly around overworked staff, waving Airheads and Pixy Stix at their parents. The floors are printed with images of jelly beans. From a distance, they look like bugs, blemishes.

I try focusing on feeling young. Little.

I want to feel good in a simple way. I want to feel like I'm taking off heavy clothes.

Downstairs, there's this strange glass case tucked behind the Fudge Bar, looking sullen and sunken-in. It's the type of case you'd see housing art projects or book reports in an elementary school hallway. The case holds jars of candy, filled and autographed by celebrities. A wooden sign swings above, reading "Famous Favorites" in an old-timey font. The tourists don't even notice it, congregating, instead, around an end-cap stacked high with Hershey Bars in glittery "I ♥ NY" packaging. A lightbulb stutters overhead. The case has an uncanny quality, making me feel seasick, unbalanced. Its glass is foggy, smeared. I see my reflection in it. The store's rainbow aesthetic reminds me of all the ways everything's become more aggressive lately: the weather, school, my brain. This case is the exact opposite: peaceful. It's just tired because nobody cares, not even the tourists.

I care. I care about peace and all the pathways to it. I press my hand on the cold glass. Maybe New York loves me differently than I was expecting. Maybe it is my teacher.

I take 5th Avenue on my walk back to Grand Central to pass the Christmas window displays: Saks, Macy's, Bergdorf Goodman. On a whim, I buy noise-canceling earbuds, almost without thinking. When I flick the switch to turn them on, the gap between my ears feels roomy. My indoors is beautiful. My indoors is snow-covered. Inside, I glisten like ice. Merry Christmas to me.

2

Grey

One morning, I noticed a bouquet of roses thrown on the ground near the gas station pump. The limp petals were beginning to brown, stems snapped clean as if tortured. It was easy to imagine the roses in motion, flinging from someone's hot hand, the pulse in their palm like the tick of a bomb. I took a picture, amused by the unexpected drama finding me on my morning commute, but, on my phone screen, the scene looked dismal and flat, a carcass.

I thought: *How are people not poets?*

I was eight when I wrote my first "grown-up" poem. It lives inside a book made of construction paper, bound with a coil of pipe cleaner. It goes like this:

Grey, the hair on an old man's head.
Grey, so lonely, so sad, and unhappy.
Grey, a cloud that covers up the sky.
Grey, a feeling that I have inside.

***

I've always written, but the Internet is what made me call myself a *writer*. In early high school, I used *Tumblr*, a trendy blogging website where teenagers, at the time, were experimenting with being frank and open. There was one blog I loved, in particular, called *Nosebleed Club*. Its contributors posted what they called "alt poetry" (—"alt," I guess, from what we read in school. 9th grade English meant picking-apart William Wordsworth and Robert Frost for weeks on end, the language brittle and aged.) *Nosebleed Club* poems were playful. They did cartwheels. They climbed trees.

My favorite of the *Nosebleed Club* contributors, Kate Monica, wrote poems with no punctuation. On my screen, they lacked gravity, the text suspended in white space. Each line crawled a distance, prompting me to widen my browser window, scroll, migrate. They were frantic poems, each skidding around a wound, doing hairpin turns.

Even when nothing thematically connected two of Kate's pieces, Kate's Kate-ness connected them. There's this quote by SZA, a musician I like. She says, "I don't give a fuck about cohesion. If you sound like you, your shit's gonna be cohesive." Kate's poems were like that.

Everything I write, too, sounds like me.

I am particular but rarely decisive. I am precious but never fussy. My writing bubbles and snaps. No matter which genre I write, it's poetry because what isn't said is as important as what is, and when it's poetry, I can't be bothered by meter or rhyme scheme. I'm too urgent. The world around me asks to be written, and it won't wait up.

After Kate Monica, my next infatuation was Tavi Gevinson, a tween prodigy in the fashion blogging world. On her blog, *The Style Rookie*, she'd write articulate paragraphs to accompany photos of her gaudy outfits. Tavi, who I still refer to by first name on a near-daily basis, as if we were friends in childhood, had an affinity for hyperlinks. She'd mention something, like—for instance—a painting that inspired her makeup, or the kitschy 80s film beginning to infiltrate her personality, then would send readers there, causing them to voyage across the web. Despite achieving the elusive, cool-girl status many of us aspired to, she preferred her work to be inclusive and rallying. For Tavi, writing was about giving. Her generosity extended to what she'd share of herself. I loved seeing her wizard out her inner world.

This was the basis of *Rookie*, a website Tavi launched in 2011 as an antidote to shallow teen magazines of the era. Each month, she gave the website a new theme: "Power," "Paradise," "Attention," "Multiplicity," "Potential," "Desire," "Utopia." Then, teens all over the world would submit work. Tavi crowned each month with her very own Editor's Letter. They were revealing and intimate, but often humorous and relaxed, like cozying up to a friend in a diner booth after a school dance. I ached to write like Tavi. I admired her ability to be meticulous, a curator. I admired her ability to set a mood.

Later, as an adult, Tavi wondered sadly if she "wasted (her) teen years art-directing her life," which makes me feel like an accomplice.

I discovered spoken word poet Jasmine Mans through a YouTube video of her piece "Gardenia." In the video, she's on a dim stage, accompanied by vocalist Jennah Bell, whose eyelids sleep as she ladles an electric guitar. They trade verses: Bell singing and Mans reciting, one nosing in after the other like synchronized swimmers. Mans and Bell were part of a "jam poetry" collective called The Strivers Row, based in Harlem. "Jam poetry," rooted in hip hop cyphers and freestyles, was defined by the collective as "slam poetry without the competitive element." This intrigued me because I didn't write poetry to win. I wrote poetry because words felt like monkey bars; I wanted to swing between them and describe the breeze. I watched "Gardenia" so many times as a teenager that I still find myself whispering it under my breath while doing chores or getting ready, like it lives in me, inextinguishable—the flame atop one of those trick birthday candles.

I sometimes wonder if every writer feels a little "off," dizzied by how much there is to take down. Being a writer and having anxiety are very related experiences in my body; they run me down and rev me up. I used to be clogged with words and unable to order them linearly. Instead, I bought big sketchbooks and filled them with magazine clippings and torn strips of newspaper. When I look at the work I made during this time, each page still feels like a complete poem. My favorite writer, Canadian essayist Durga Chew-Bose, once mentioned she "love(s) the idea of brevity ... because the world is inconclusive." I think, often, a poem is an utterance.

It's the click of a tongue or the wiggle of a tooth. Every poem I write inches closer to my center.

I couldn't cut-the-cord from Maggie Nelson's memoir *The Argonauts*. I snuck it into my most boring class and read it every time the professor looked down at his lecture notes. I read it on the "quiet floor" of the Hunter College library, a place that always felt still in a sickly way, like a doctor's office. *The Argonauts* sizzled in the most monotonous places.

It's about Nelson, a pregnant woman startled by her changing body, and her partner, a trans man beginning testosterone injections. Stylistically, *The Argonauts* shifts from personal narrative to academic writing. Nelson wedges quotes from theorist Judith Butler (who famously coined the phrase "gender is performance") in the margins. Butler's research validates the couple's experiences with in-betweenness. Grey area. I wasn't pregnant, nor did I wish to transition, but it seemed like language failed to hold all of us similarly. *Grey was a feeling that we had inside.*

Around the same time, I read Gertrude Stein, a poet who arranged words so that their meanings could be conjured through their associations with one another, rather than through their dictionary definitions. In short, she invented a grammar. In *Tender Buttons*, a collection published back in 1914, which explores the tension of women's roles in the home, her writing is purposefully puzzling and—almost—illegible. However, its lack of sense creates sense. Poets.org calls *Tender Buttons* "a spectacular failure, a collection of confusing gibberish, and an intentional hoax."

I first heard the word "failure" used in this context in a

book called *The Queer Art of Failure* by Jack Halberstam, assigned to me in a Gender Studies class. The book argues that "failing" at norms, expectations, and boundaries is how we, as humans, can push through to the transformative, abundant, and creative. We can achieve freedom (from the prison of heteronormativity, among other things) by "failing." Since the 1970s, Queer Theory scholars have argued that if enough of us "fail," it will be revealed how many of our norms are socially constructed and, thus, unnecessary.

I believe that inside a metaphor is the world. The language we're given, by doctors and therapists and well-meaning friends, is never enough. It's too tight at the shoulders, baggy loose on the legs. I want to write my brain like language is new, like language has fallen into my lap, and I'm surprised by it.

I want to fail spectacularly.

***

Michael, one of my first students, talked about winning an Academy Award like his name was already in the envelope waiting. He asked to use our classroom as a set one lunch period. I watched him pose the bodies of his actors (friends, with call times and free pizza) for a short film he was making. I heard him say, "Thanks for your help, man. When I win my Oscar, I'll thank you in my speech. We can pop champagne and shit."

Michael bent thoughtfully over a notebook, crossing off completed shots. He told me his film was "about juxtaposition." This was funny and fitting since I had just begun noticing the two selves he held inside, the dissonance between them. There was this pompous, blustering celebrity-to-be and a careful, intense artist. I always feel freed by conflict. Michael in motion was beautiful to witness.

***

When I tell people I write, they want to know what I write *about*, as if the answer's obvious. There are two quotes I like: Tracy Clayton's "Writing is exactly like detangling your hair," and Adrienne Rich's "Poems are like dreams. In them, you put what you don't know you know." Even the act of writing itself, I think, can only be explained figuratively. It's impossible to get exact enough, otherwise.

An old poetry professor once told me I am a modern-day Frank O'Hara, for I write about nothing (action, plot, situation-wise) and everything (thematically, emotionally). At the time, I was workshopping a piece about a girl in my hometown who unexpectedly passed away when she was a high school senior. I hardly knew her, and our connection was peripheral; we shared a mutual friend or two. However, the town looked different when she left it, like I could constantly see the jagged edge of where she was torn out. I wrote this specific poem to explain how it felt, to drive past different things and see this hole. Where else can you describe that feeling—*the absence of*—but in a poem? How else can you describe what's invisible besides describing what's around it?

I had another poetry professor who critiqued in a way that felt humid and smothering. She didn't give me room to find the stories in my underarms and bellybutton. Once, I couldn't hold it together as she tore into my poem and sobbed over the long conference table I shared with my peers. After class, she wanted to speak with me in the hallway and hugged me. The following week, she showed us the 2014 film, *Whiplash*, about a jazz musician and his punitive, strict band director. The film culminates in a scene where the musician realizes the only way he'll succeed is if he succumbs to the harsh instruction and listens to the one person "pushing him." I went home feeling upset and confused.

In my head, I'd always like to keep writing and abuse unlinked. I'd like for writing to have a clean, strong membrane. I once attended a Q&A with the poet Tommy Pico. When asked for his best writing advice, he eventually arrived at "build laterally" and urged us to dislodge success from an MFA, from publication, from instructors' approval. I found his advice more abstract than precise, but I allow it to sit with me, and I find it comforting. The only thing I value more than the personal is the communal. I am only *me* because I am not *you*. We are only *us* because we happened upon each other. All of this is poetry.

I think I would still be a writer even if I didn't have a single reader.

Writing feels like hunger, like searching. This isn't a bad thing—as I find weighing answers more fulfilling than finding them—but I am often exhausted by it. A major red flag is when a newborn idea feels like a can-of-worms rather than a warm, deep ocean.

A healthy "writer's life" is about accepting what is and what isn't and what could be.

I have made futile attempts to contain my desire to write. Like many people, I have tried to shove writing into a daily timeslot, so it gets sequestered between—say—class and a dentist appointment. I always try to tame it, but I can't. Desire is an animal.

3

Angels

I'm seated next to a nine-year-old boy and his mom at Ariana Grande's 2019 world tour. The boy—peppy, up to his forearm in a bag of cotton candy—keeps talking to me, seemingly unfazed by my age and stranger-ness. (Are there really "strangers" at concerts? It's like just going to the event tethers us.) There's a pre-show playlist cascading over the burgeoning crowd at Madison Square Garden: TLC's "No Scrubs," Lauryn Hill's "Doo Wop (That Thing)," lots of Britney. My ears adjust to the boom of the shuddering speakers. I close my eyes and imagine Ariana with her glam team backstage, warming up her voice to Whitney's "I'm Every Woman" while stylists slip sequined barrettes around the stalk of her ponytail, one too many.

In the music video for her track "7 rings," Ariana lays on the ground beside a campy Rapunzel-length ponytail. In behind-the-scenes clips, she complains of how the prop yanks at her scalp. Several crew members must carry it behind her like the train on a wedding gown. It's so satirical—all of "7 rings" is; the song, when in context with the rest of its respective album, exposes how unfulfilling money and materialism can be.

Ariana's ponytail has always felt like a symbol. It's too long for its own good, and she comes close to tripping on it. It gets stuck in her lipgloss on stage. In a skit on *The Tonight Show Starring Jimmy Fallon*, it comes to life, reaches for various objects around the room like a third hand. She even owns a baseball cap with a hole scissored in the crown to allow for the way it sprouts directly upward, its freakish height. Ariana laughs at herself ahead of being laughed at, a preemptive measure. There's a comedy to her career; it's raunchy in a cheap, unserious way. She parodies herself.

There are only a few things Ariana gets criticized for, and the ponytail is one of them, both for its excessiveness and the way it borrows from Black women's styles. Still, she rarely switches it up, hugs the stringy hair extensions around her small frame like a blanket. Her stage style—big and pink and glittery—feels vulnerable, like an obvious costume.

Days after Ariana's former boyfriend, rapper Mac Miller, overdosed and died in 2018, paparazzi photos surfaced showing her wandering around Manhattan in a daytime rainstorm, grief smeared all over her face. Her hair extensions were gone, the toddler-length locks beneath them gathered in two limp pigtails. She was—at once—totally unrecognizable and exactly how you'd imagine her to be, for the glam, the mythology of Ariana Grande, is loosely stuck on.

I'm grateful for the conversation with this young kid because, although I enjoy attending concerts alone (it's freeing!), there's always a period of unease before the artist begins their set. With the arena lights on, I feel very seen, caught-in-the-act of doing something "beneath me." I recently received my college diploma and, while walking at graduation, felt loss leap through me, haunted by the idea that I'd have to begin letting parts of me go. After devoting so much time to my studies, I wouldn't want people to discredit my intellect because I'm—so vocally—an "obsessive fan" of pop stars.

The boy's mother asks me to take their picture. He holds a wad of cotton candy at the camera; they say "thank u, next!" instead of "Cheese!" quoting Grande's most famous track. Sugar crusts on the boy's lips.

When I hand back the woman's phone, she whispers discreetly that her son got bullied at school for dancing to an Ariana song at the Winter talent show. Then, aloud, she says, "We're going to get her attention tonight!" the way someone would promise their child a visit from the Tooth Fairy. "Right, Ethan? When she pulls you up on stage, will you dance for her, or will you get too shy?"

The boy nods eagerly. "I'll dance!"

I feel a buzz of excitement, knowing *I'm* sitting close enough to the stage that there's a chance Ariana might see *me*, too.

I feel it, then feel stupid. This kid—Ethan—is a seed, and I am a flower. I do not need someone to come along and water me. I already exist.

A Madonna song fills the arena. I hum along, scouting the nearby rows for people my age. Some of them stand alone, too, swaying to the music, eating overpriced hot dogs from the lobby. I can get so caught up in thinking every feeling I have is unique to me.

Ethan pokes at my wrist, waiting for me to make eye contact before delivering a line of dialogue from the "thank u, next" music video. In a kid-like way, he misquotes a joke alluding to Ariana's failed engagement with *Saturday Night Live* comic Pete Davidson. Ariana lets fans feel privy to a lot of her private relationships. When she broke it off with Davidson, several friends texted me, asking my thoughts, which, in a way, felt nice, like they were saying "I love you" to me.

A family sitting near us gives Ethan one of their extra glow-sticks. He pretends it's a microphone and lip-syncs for them, wagging a finger in the air at the high notes. He's precocious and forward in a way I never was. Once, I'd seen a video of Ariana at his age, starring in a Boca Raton production of *Annie*. In it, an interviewer from the local news pulls her aside backstage, pushing a chunky 90s camera in her face. She squirms for a moment, then flashes a smile beneath the tight curls of her red wig. The reporter asks if she was nervous before auditioning for the lead role. She replies, with disconcerting desire, "No? It was fun," then laughs, clamping a hand over her mouth in regret. It's a nervous laugh that I recognize from her recent red carpet interviews, similar to a pot bubbling-over. Ariana overcompensates for her discomfort around the press by talking franticly. In recent years, she only lets one person—a friend, Zach Sang—interview her. She has become more reclusive.

Ethan tells the family who gave him the glow-stick that he wants to be famous. He savors the word as he says it.

Not long ago, Ariana live-streamed on Instagram for the first time in a long time and abruptly signed off within minutes. Afterward, she posted a meandering rant, claiming her Instagram follower count causes her paranoia, how she wouldn't wish two hundred million followers on her worst enemy. I imagined her bent in the heat of a spotlight, sweating.

At one point, I cut my own Instagram follower count down dramatically, feeling a sudden, blazing connection to the remaining friends and acquaintances. I wish I could carry that relief on a torch to Ariana, but I am greedy and nosy and wouldn't want to lose my spot in her world.

***

"So, why are *you* here?" Ethan's mom asks.

I pretend the question doesn't make me feel homeless. "Ariana puts on a great show!" I say, with a foreign blandness and restraint.

The answer satisfies her. Since Ariana's a household name, many of her concert attendees are casual listeners. They stand unmoved for the entire show, then buoyantly scream the lyrics to whichever #1 hit she pulls out as an encore—a solid night-out.

I'm surprised when she doesn't press me further. She turns toward Ethan, who's begun playing Concentration 64 with a teen girl sitting behind us, his easy sociability frightening and admirable. I flirt with the idea of interrupting and telling them I *know* Ariana, which is a lie and a truth at once.

I first heard Ariana sing on the soundtrack of the short-lived Broadway show, *13*, which had a score tackling the trials and tribulations of puberty. It opened in 2007. I was a theater-obsessed 6th grader. Naturally, it hit home.

Perhaps, it was the first piece of pop culture that arrived to me alone. It was low-brow—a cringe comedy—but I loved it with earnest intensity. Electric guitars sliced each airtight show tune to suggest angst. Teenage Ariana had a supporting role: Charlotte, the school gossip. She soloed on the show's finale number, "Brand New You." Her voice, shoutier then, soared across complicated notes with dexterity. I welcomed her confidence because it felt earned.

My fascination with *13, The Musical* bled into a summer vacation of something akin to research. I honed in on Ariana, who stirred something in my chest. I dug through her relatively small online archives, spending most of my July and August on a YouTube channel called "osnapitzari," where the Broadway actress had been posting videos for years. I watched them for hints of her personality, which often mirrored or became mine. I remember noting her worship-like reverence for divas like Celine Dion and Mariah Carey, her mental library of early-2000s sleepover films. She'd rattle off impressions with her much older half-brother, Frankie, a theatrical, goofy adult who, at the time, played Boots in a touring production of *Dora The Explorer: Live!* Friends reoccurred in her videos like series regulars on a sitcom. I knew them by name: Misha, Alexa, Courtney. Aaron, in particular, was her partner-in-crime. In the years leading up to Ariana's Broadway debut, the two created a multi-part sci-fi series called *Freaky Forever*. They'd play all the characters, doing voices. The editing was clippy and amateur. Nothing about it was cool. In fact, it's something I probably would have made fun of my own classmates for doing.

Madison Square Garden simmers. Frank Ocean's "Chanel" fills the arena, lowering the temperature. I've always wanted Frank and Ariana to collaborate. They have a similar precision to their vocals. I sometimes think Ariana's voice sounds like a bell: direct and clear. It reaches into me.

Ethan sticks the glow-stick sideways in his mouth, causing his cheeks to protrude, desperately trying to make the teens behind us laugh. It's funny, to me, that he and I are both so attached to Ariana. When I was Ethan's age, people frequently described me as an "old soul." I anxiously yearned for praise of all kinds, and this particular type rendered me *interesting*. I replayed Avril Lavigne CDs until the discs skipped and memorized Hilary Duff lyrics for playground *American Idol* games, but I was not a fan of people for their person. Seemingly, every adult in my life (inadvertently or not) told me this was something immature kids did. I wouldn't let myself indulge in these fervent emotions, so I choked them out, and disposed of them quickly, as if they were naughty. Once, a friend of mine camped out to meet Justin Bieber. I remember regurgitating a phrase that's been run-to-the-ground at this point, which dismisses a lot of the nuance in the fan/artist relationship: *He's not going to marry you!*

When I was in 8th grade, Ariana booked a role on Nickelodeon's *Victorious*. I tuned in to the premiere, slightly embarrassed to select the channel, which I'd parted from a few years prior, feeling "too old" for it. The premiere followed the *Kids Choice Awards*, which, particularly, felt like such a sting. (At the time, I felt so far out of the show's target demographic. However, this year, they put *Victorious* on Netflix, and I learned that most of my peers were also watching it back then. Suddenly, there was this mass nostalgia for something I mistakenly thought I experienced alone.) Ariana played Cat Valentine, an eccentric student at the show's Hollywood Arts High School, with hair "the color of red-velvet cupcakes." The dye damaged her natural hair so profoundly that, as the series progressed, she began wearing stiff, firetruck-colored wigs.

Most episodes of *Victorious* featured a musical number. I Tweeted at Ariana the night Nickelodeon announced she'd be singing on the show for the first time. She wrote back almost immediately, thanking me, calling me "sweet." I was sleeping over at my grandparents' house that night, still too young to stay home alone while my parents went on a weekend trip. I fell asleep with a smile pressed against the pull-out couch. Months later, when I turned 13, she direct-messaged me "happy birthday" unprompted, even before my friends from school did.

Ariana and costar Liz Gillies were housemates at the time. Liz, a natural comic, would make Ariana laugh so much she'd look like her father, a *Fox News*-obsessed fisherman. I watched any video they made together with an air of devotion. In them, Ariana smiled, unsexy, genuine; her voice would flatline, deepen into a grunt.

Ariana's perceived speaking voice is as controversial as her ponytail. She tends to push it up into its highest register. It's sing-song-y, a reminder that she can carry a tune, but it can be annoying, a "baby voice." Sometimes, I wonder if this way of speaking is a nervous habit, too, or—further—a coping mechanism. If people perceive her as cute and innocent, who'd dare hurt her? When she's *really* off-camera—not on a late-night show, accepting an award, or promoting one of her fragrances on Instagram—her voice is throaty and boyish. It cracks. She heaves curse words. She can be whatever the space needs, a shapeshifter. There's wisdom in her ability to skirt public perception, outsmart it, and I see it. I do.

This is what I mean when I say I *know* her.

***

It's not like I don't have a personal life. That's the stereotype—right?—that people who love celebrities are filling a void? I always had someone to sit with at lunch in middle school, someone to creep the mall with on Friday nights. Now, in my 20s, I have friends who create walls when the world feels too big and open windows when it feels too small. I have fruitful and snug relationships. They are messy, vibrant, and lived. I have community and mentors and intimacy and family. Ariana is not a placeholder. I already have *so much*.

However, I'm tough on myself and extremely sensitive. Loving Ariana is a reprieve because she *doesn't* know me. It's the only relationship I'll ever have that'll be perfect. It lives in my brain; every part of it comes from me.

I recently watched the film *Ingrid Goes West*, starring Aubrey Plaza and Elizabeth Olsen, about a lonely woman obsessed with an LA influencer. Her allegiance to this stranger online eventually drives her to move across the country and restart her life in a way that will increase the chances of them meeting. It's supposed to be a cautionary tale.

On my way to the bathroom, I walk past fans of all ages, many of them aiming to dress like Grande, Forever 21 knock-offs of her recent looks. There are little girls in homemade t-shirts caked with puffy paint, their mothers sipping diligently at plastic cups of wine from the arena's bar. My mood shifts from pride to annoyance, then back again. It's my second time seeing Ariana at The Garden. She's been touring nonstop for the past ten years, frequently speaking of her workaholism, her inability to slow down. Sometimes, I hear fear in her voice, and I'm unsure where it's coming from. Is it *my* fear or hers?

The arena is sold-out and begins to look like it as everyone puzzles into their places. I can't stop thinking about Ethan, a boy for whom Ariana is obviously providing some lifeline, and I feel gratitude for the way she's touched him in the way she's touched me. Then, I sneer at the idea, like a possessive girlfriend. Does he know her weirdest interests? —how much she loves Halloween? —how she plays *Mario Kart* when she can't sleep? —her lifelong celebrity crush on Jim Carrey?

I pass by a merchandise stand on the way to the bathroom and buy a t-shirt, chuckling at myself, how easy it is to slip into the territory of that girl from *Ingrid Goes West*, imagining an intimacy that isn't there, becoming vicious with it.

I have to squeeze the t-shirt into a clear plastic purse I bought specifically for tonight. Since a terrorist attack occurred at one of Ariana's concerts in Manchester, England late 2017, killing 23 fans, she's been requiring all ticket-holders to enter her shows with see-through bags for security purposes.

At one point, she posted (then quickly deleted) a scan done by her doctor that showed her brain lit up in a fiery glow, overactive, scorched—the physical impact of PTSD. She positioned the brain-scan next to a healthy brain diagram, the contrast sharp, sad.

At one point, I asked Twitter to notify me when she Tweeted, feeling concerned for her wellbeing, like, if I could catch something fast enough, I'd be able to help her, like I could come over and sit with her on hard nights. Eventually, I felt useless and embarrassed, so I turned the notifications off.

***

The show's openers are fine. Ethan stands on his chair, arms up, spreading his palms wide like he's trying to catch the music. I lack his energy and feel old, a cramp in my lower back. The weight of my life sits in me.

Finally, Ariana's voice severs the arena, singing "raindrops (an angel cried)," the intro off her record *Sweetener*. Suddenly, I'm up on my chair, too. Ethan and I yell and scream.

I am a fan, and I am part of something.

It's not until the setlist reaches "breathin'," a vague single about coping with anxiety, nothing particularly groundbreaking, that I realize I'm crying. I'm crying out all of these stuck tears, ingrown, in me. I'm crying and crying, and then Ariana has walked to my end of the arena, and she's staring at me.

The shape of her eyes is familiar. We sing the second verse as a duet. There is only my voice and hers. Her ponytail is brittle up-close, fibrous, like a wig you'd buy at Party City. The air smells winter fresh. I am young again, lying in bed on my belly, watching her through the screen of my iPod Touch. She is a cacoon. I metamorphize. The roof of the arena crumbles, and we're flying: two people—the same. We are both angels, our thick wings lapping at the world.

Then, she walks away, and I am still me.

4

Solar Eclipse

My ponytail swings as I stretch my hamstring. The dance studio smells like Clorox. It's always cold until we start moving.

Gloria barges through the glass door, bringing her day with her. "Get this! Richard wants to go out to the Hamptons this weekend, but I already promised the grandkids I'd come to this little party they're having to watch the solar eclipse. I'm always telling him, 'If you love the beach so much, you should have married *the Hamptons* instead of me!'" With a huff, she chucks her tote bag near our mountain of belongings. Gloria's in her 60s. My gym hosts Dance Fitness in the mid-afternoon, a 3 PM slot retired women like. I like the anonymity of dancing with them, how I can sort of disappear into my body's movement. However, they all demand attention as if they were never taught to fold. I usually admire outspoken women, but I feel a generational wall between us. They use their voices to critique and complain rather than advocate and uplift.

Gloria's best friend is Mary. They have matching jazz shoes. Gossip fireworks between them as they roll onto their toes and crick their necks. This is their usual routine. Mary has a sloppy tattoo of Mickey Mouse on her wrinkled ankle, which peeks out whenever her yoga pants ride up. Something about it feels like seeing the costumed character at Disney World remove his head.

I'm observant in the way that always makes you feel let down.

The dance instructor busily toggles the volume switch on the stereo, causing a sugary pop song to crash over the room. Mary speaks up to compete with the noise. "Did you buy those special glasses?"

"For what?"

"Watching the eclipse. If you look directly at it, it can damage your eyesight."

"Oh, yes. My daughter bought a pack of 100. She invited all the neighborhood kids. She spoils those boys—let me tell you."

Mary shakes her head in disbelief, a vein pulsing above her eyebrow. "Millennial parenting," she mutters. "It's something else. My daughters are like that too. Liz did presents for Halloween. I was like—what's next? Cake on Presidents' Day?"

Gloria's mouth falls open in mock distress; then, she collects herself. "You have to admit—it's pretty cool that we get to see the eclipse this time around. Who would've thought two old broads like us would have a "first" to look forward to?" Their laughs modulate.

Mary singles me out with her pointer finger from the knot of women—little lumps on the floor, tying their shoelaces, stretching. "*This one* gets to see an eclipse before she graduates high school!"

My eyes roll before I can stop them. "I'm a high school teacher, actually," I lie. I'm not even certified yet. My student-teaching placement starts next week. I'm just angry that someone can see the teenager in me. I'm 21, and adolescence feels unshakeable.

"A teacher! Wow." Gloria winks at me. "Lucky boys."

***

I think I knew when I was 9. The knowledge sounded like a siren at first. A friend's older sister checked the tag on my shirt to see where I got it from and glazed a hand softly on my neck. Stars ripped open where her skin touched mine. Within minutes, I was calling my mom to pick me up. This older girl's bedroom door was magnetic thereafter as I passed it, my socks slow in the carpeted hallway.

It wasn't until I was 14 that the knowledge voweled in my mouth. I birthed the word alone, under the covers, up too late. The birth was messy and painful. Muddy colors splattered my sheets. I cleaned up my secret, still sore. Everything was dry by morning.

It was a lot at first. To know myself.

I don't feel volcanic anymore. I've told my friends, family members. Ironically, this part felt like a ticking-off of boxes—tedious, almost. It was nothing in comparison to the flames I put out within me, a whack-a-mole of each alarm that wailed. Shame is layered. It's hard to identify the source.

But loving women is beginning to sound like water—like

the inside of a well, like a kitchen sink, like a glass on the nightstand. My truth is crawling closer and closer to home. It stands by my bedside. My truth wears pajamas.

***

When I dry myself off after a shower, I always start with my ears. This feeling reminds me of childhood, leaving the community pool with my grandmother, who'd spray my hair from behind with a fruity L'Oréal detangler. I catch a bead of water trilling down the bridge of my nose, like a raindrop chasing down a car window. I hang the towel on my face. I think: *it's nice to be in the dark for a minute.* I exhale.

When my head is dry, I swing the towel around my back, fly it like a cape, use its corners to run along my jawline, touching places I sometimes forget to engage with: the shoulders, the chest—an area responsible for my whole nervous system, the way I'm wound. I pet myself.

I pluck a small hair from my breast. My midsection is graceful and feminine: a relaxed stomach and hips that slope out. I dry my abdomen. I am soft, and it's all over. It's my skin and my heart. A few tiny stretch marks gather on the side of my leg: ring-shaped. I peel and peel.

I place a hand over my belly button and let everything rise and fall beneath me. I am an island and the weather is balmy. My body blues with desire. I crawl down into myself. My breath is heavy and hot. There is nothing I can't do on my own.

***

The eclipse is tomorrow.

"I bet President Trump will look directly at it," Mary from Dance Fitness bellows. When she cackles, I notice one of her teeth is fanged. A few ladies bend deep into their stretches to avoid having to agree or argue.

Gloria, who once claimed Donald Trump is "who Jesus would have voted for," scoffs, playfully punching her friend on the arm. I've noticed these women talk about politics in a way that's aggressive in tone but ultimately detached. "I can't wait to see what Melania wears. She always dresses so elegantly at White House events."

"I'll give her that."

Together, they swish the hems on their workout tops. "I'd do anything for those beautiful gowns," Gloria sighs. I watch in the mirror as her sandpaper legs waltz back and forth.

"We all know why a woman like her ended up with Trump!" Mary looks broadly at the group, mischief in her eyes, begging for a reaction. She raises a hand and rubs her thumb and middle finger together. "*Cha-ching! Cha-ching!* Gold digger!" The skin under her arm swings loose like jello.

"Hey, Mary!" Gloria joins the show, basking in the growing audience of eyes. "I'm just happy we no longer have a First Lady who looks like a man!"

"Are you talking about Michelle?"

"Remember her arms?" Gloria flexes her muscles. She blows air into her cheeks.

"Oh, shut up. You know what? Melania can wear all the gowns in the world and still look tacky to me. Her attitude is tacky."

Gloria snorts. "At least Hillary Clinton didn't win. She dresses like a lesbian." The word clots the air. It smells. Finally, everyone laughs. Mary throws an arm around her friend.

Our instructor switches on music, drowning out the conversation. I walk to my place on the floor. Within a minute, we're all dancing. Our shoes clap the wood floor. I am invisible.

***

I have these recurring dreams where I'm holding hands with a girl I like. They feel so great that, when I wake up, I can never decide whether or not I enjoyed them. There's a certain whiplash in losing the handhold. Morning snatches it.

A lot of girls get to be The Girl. She's only an outline. When I recognize a feature, like a birthmark or a dimple or a slang word said too much, when my dreams give me a hint, I wake up frantically reaching for my phone. I want to text whoever it was. I want to say, "Hey! You were The Girl last night!" as if this information will woo her, but nobody cares about other people's dreams.

When I try to hold my own hand, I feel disappointed by the lack of electricity. Even when I close my eyes and wish and wish and wish. Even when I fantasize and pretend I am half-me and half-Her. Nothing.

I want to hold a hand. I want to know if it will solve anything in me.

There's so much to wonder about. Will her hand be smaller than mine? I think that's nice. I think that will make me feel like I have everything I need. Or will I be the small one? That's nice too—to be safe in the stretch of someone else. Will she wear a bracelet that clinks against her wrist like music? Will she have short, clean nails? A manicure? Will I see my hands in her hands? Will she be a mirror? Do I want a mirror?

When I sleep, I don't have to think so much. Sleep is a renaissance. It cracks me open.

I work part-time at a café. We watch the eclipse out back, in the staff parking lot.

Noelle works in an art gallery a few stores down. She says she's with our group because we have cookies and the good glasses. Her hair is long and smells like berries, blonde at the ends from the sun. She keeps grabbing my wrist to tell me things. Her eyes look like lily pads or cucumbers. I like when she leans in.

I am ripe with a crush and it sours quick. I wonder why the devil needs an advocate. Fear is a safety net I never wanted. Still, when I see Noelle, it's like a recess period. It's like Spring Break. Today, she brings me a pair of these homemade earrings she makes and sells—gold wire hugging two pieces of amethyst. I say, "Thank you. They're so cool," and I mean, "Can you make me these forever? Can I watch you bent over the table with pliers, your nose scrunched? Can your hobby live in my home? Can we be a *we*?"

My coworker Harry tinkers with his camera and tripod, side-eying a NASA live stream pulled up on his phone. "If I screw up this shot, I don't know if I'll ever live it down."

Noelle smirks. "Noone wants to see a photo of the eclipse."

"The scientific community does."

"Harry, you're a barista," Noelle deadpans. "The only thing

the *scientific community* wants from you is an iced latte on their way into work."

"At least I can make a latte," he teases back. Noelle keeps coming in while Harry and I are working and, if we're slow, we let her fumble with the espresso maker. She gets nervous when steaming the milk. Last week, she burned her hand. I pulled her into the dim staff bathroom, and she watched as I fished a bandaid out of our first aid kit, stuck it slowly to her palm. She didn't flinch, her eyes curious, her hand pushing up into mine.

Harry knows I like her. After she left that day, he went, "Noelle, huh? No wonder she comes in here so much." Then, he patted my back like a father on TV.

I'm sitting on the hood of my car, and she lifts herself next to me. We can't decide where to put our hands. We redlight/greenlight. "The magic part of the eclipse is watching it in person, remembering who you were with, so you can tell your kids and stuff," she says. I nod, a sort of pain in my mouth.

There's a blitz of noise on Harry's phone—excited scientists chattering. It's happening. There's a chill, but I can't tell if it's outside or inside my body. "Glasses on, everyone!" Harry yelps, nudging my manager and a few customers who've gathered with us. He looks boyish, bouncing on his toes in excitement. Noelle and I lean back like this is a bed, our elbows deciding whether or not to be brave.

The moon's stuck in front of the sun. Harry cries out in joy as applause freckles the parking lot. Noelle looks at me, smiling. Her teeth glow in the dark. We are so close.

"I feel like crying," I tell her—whispered.

"That's okay."

"Oh."

"Yeah. It's really beautiful," Noelle says, so I don't have to look.

I want to change the question from "Why are my edges sharper than the holes I need to slip into?" to "Do I have ancestors that loved like me?" I want to find them in the sky.

I think I am the eclipse.

In me, the sun and moon sleep together. In me, the sky is a radiant dark.

I scissor open my feelings to let the air out. My truth pops like balloons.

***

On my first day of student teaching, I stand at the front of the room, baby-faced, with bruises on my knees because I am still clumsy and a triangle of zits on my chin because I am still hormonal. I enamor the students because I'm in college. A group of girls hover over my desk at the end of class to ask me questions:

"What's it like?"

"Do people hang out on *the quad*?"

"Do you drink at parties?"

"Could I get into Harvard if I'm failing science? I've always loved Harvard since *Legally Blonde*."

I answer them dutifully until, "Do you have a boyfriend?" which makes me look down at my computer, picking lint from the keyboard with a fingernail.

Quickly, I say, "No. No boyfriend."

"Why are you blushing?" the same girl says, her eyes round and excited. "Is there a boy you like?"

"Is there a boy *you* like?" I joke, putting her in the hot seat. The girls all laugh, moving closer and closer to me, like they are planets in my orbit. I feel their warmth. And they are young. And they are the future. And so I drop, "Actually, I'm gay," like it's a feather.

"Oh. Well, do you have a girlfriend?" The bell rings and students flood the hallway—a gush, relief.

"Working on it," I laugh. I try out, in my head, how the moment would've gone if I'd said, "Yeah. Her name is Noelle." I think it would feel like flowers. I'm going to ask her out. Courage is a side-effect of hope. "Get going. I don't want you to be late for your next class."

When they're out the door, I hear one go, "Oh my God! We have to tell Maddie. She'll be so happy there's a lesbian teacher."

After school, Maddie—who has a different English teacher—stops by my classroom just to say hi, to sit in my light for a second. It makes me think of how I would linger on my bike near the house of the only gay couple on my street—two older women with no knowledge of me. It's not like I'd ever go in, but I'd break, and my wheels would slow, and I'd feel better.

I'm falling for myself. A feeling can burst from my brain, and I can catch it, squeeze out its juice, make it into words on a page, standing militant, orderly, perfect. I can fight fires with all that language, scorching the threat of pathlessness. I can create space. I can help wash the sheets.

In my dream last night, I pointed a ladder up at the clouds and climbed. I bounced on the sun like a trampoline.

5

Sandwiches

The cashier at Target helps a customer shoplift. Together, they hurriedly shove cans of soup and a pack of diapers into a reusable bag. The shoplifter, a nervous woman, mashes the keypad with a practiced seriousness, like a child playing Grocery Store. Mouth full of apology, the cashier shushes me with a twitch of the eyes as she pretends to hit buttons on her screen. I think I'm supposed to feel an itch of guilt for noticing, but I don't. There's church in my body. It's all so odd and tender.

I think I love both of them.

To be honest, this is the first positive thought I've had all day.

The clouds send down a corny rainstorm as I push my shopping cart through the lot afterward. Thankfully, I have an umbrella with me. I have this habit, lately, of forgetting where I parked. I'm too in-my-head, this world secondary to that one. The wheels on my cart spit a puddle at my shins.

"All good?" a man asks, unloading his baby from the backseat of a Honda Civic. I immediately find him sort of frustrating. He has a cross-shaped nick on his chin from shaving and hair sticky with gel.

I fish for my keyring in my tote bag and thumb it several times to sound the alarm. The baby waves at me, and I decide the rain isn't corny; it's just sad. It's all sad—this and that and that and that, and now a baby is here.

"This little guy loves the rain," the man continues, taking my thoughtful quiet as an invitation to talk. "I wish I could get him this excited about taking a bath!" The baby squints, unamused, tugging his dad's collar. I hate when parents speak for their children. Maybe somewhere in my brain, I remember being born, the sound still tucked there. It must've been intense, a white coat doctor eye-level as I took my first scream, nobody asking, "how do *you* feel, baby?" Being without language.

"He's cute," I say. Three birthmarks gather into a nest above his left eyebrow. His fingernails look like seashells, translucent and glassy. He's so fragile. I wonder if he gets placed in front of the TV while the news roars? Does it get caught behind his eardrums? Has anyone told him they're going to make the world better for him? I try to communicate this with my eyes, but there's rain in the way, and I'm not feeling articulate.

The man opens his mouth to continue the conversation, but I say, "Bye!" I watch the word cross from me to him, sizzling invisibly like an electric fence. Lately, conversations feel like bumper cars. Am I out-of-practice? I spend a lot of time alone right now. Alone is an awning.

The rain won't end—angry on my car windows. Slumped

in the front seat, I keep thinking of all the friends I don't see anymore, each name heavy like a wet towel as I take it out of my head. I am a people-person. I am.

***

In the morning, I go for a walk. They said this would help. Blue TV seeps from a second-floor window. Some neighborhood kid eats a popsicle over the trash bin. It's summer, but everything is quiet. Silence rivers between my ears. My neighborhood comes of age. It's green at the knee and fuschia at the hip. Do flowers grow brighter the less we see them? That's a gentle realization. Like realizing I am more interested in heaven than God. It allows me to relax.

Our lawn has bedhead. I get the mail and sift through it, criss-cross in the knotty grass. I scrape a stick at a caterpillar tangled in a curl, brown and thick as a child's eyelash. My friend Beth has decided to write letters to me. Her pen is heavy and present on the stationery and she places little stickers on the envelope. It feels like we are sitting together.

At night, the mosquitoes come out, but my family lights a citronella candle. We put our elbows on the outdoor furniture, eating off the barbeque, patting a palm on the rear of a ketchup bottle. An airplane is clunky in the sky above, which makes us Google a clip of The Challenger exploding. It's like one thing leads to another. I mention a celebrity, and someone brings up the time they got "canceled." Everyone chews with their mouths open. The conversation swivels and spins. I swallow my food as I hear it slip-and-slide. "Nobody can say anything anymore. Cancel culture is a witch hunt!" I believe accountability and criticism are descendants of care, but I choose to think my words for later. The mosquitoes eat my ankles, a punishment for keeping the peace. I guard my perspective tighter. I save it for when it will be more effective. One cannot build a house until the ground is smooth. Feeling without thinking only results in more noise.

***

There's a lot going on. Just because the news is in my belly doesn't mean it has to make me sick. I look to moments of chaos, not as the tightening of the air around me but as the eye of a needle, through which I can see pain. I am unflinching as I take stock. What balm do I have? What salve? Who can I touch with the softest hands they've felt in a while? Who can I speak to for whom my voice will cut clear through the noise?

I think I care about every human, even the "bad" ones. My mom says that's a very religious thing to think, which is confusing. This is just *me*. I am spacious and without rules. I let everyone in.

Are we actually safer in the world as it currently exists than we would be in a different one? Who is harmed by the myth of comfort? What exactly *is* the threat? Why is violence excused if it's in response to violence?

I cut at the root. What is anger, anyway, but a tiredness?

I turn off the news for now. There's a lot going on.

***

I wait for the dark to tell me I'm allowed to go to bed. There's a sleep hypnosis video on YouTube I like, for when my body is starfished, stiff against the mattress. In the comments section, people disclose their battles with insomnia and grief. It's cloudy down there, each paragraph bloated and wistful. I always find myself reading the replies, each a canopy of comforting messages from other users. I wonder, briefly: *how helpful is it when the-blind-leads-the-blind?* I mean, we all clicked on the same video, didn't we? But then, I realize this is the world I want, where nobody has to be an expert in order to be helpful. I light candles behind my eyelids and pray others fall asleep tonight, which lets me drift off, too.

***

Beth's New Year's Resolution was to start buying herself flowers. When we hang out, finally, we sift through baskets of bouquets in front of the deli, her on her knees to get a good look.

I should have made a New Year's Resolution. I've been wanting to learn to knit. If I knit, maybe I could learn to love my hands even when they're not doing enough. My grandmother used to teach me as a child. She'd step away to refill the stained lap of her teacup, and I'd look back at the measly "scarf" or "blanket" snaking from my needles, embarrassed. When she'd return, I'd say I was bored. I have never stuck with things that I am not good at. Beth does, though, and she gets really good at them.

I watch her study the bouquets. I don't know the names of

flowers like she does. Should this be my New Year's Resolution? Will it help me grow downward? Beth has a sturdiness to her. A reliability. She is the type to pack a snack for later, to keep an extra hair tie on her wrist. When I am around her, I feel less like I am floating away.

Beth chooses a bouquet and cheats out toward the sun to see it from a new angle. We agree it's perfect, each petal a moody purple. "Where are you going to put them?" I ask. I mean—which room? Which shelf?

"Where the light hits," she responds.

I picture the hardwood floors of my own bedroom, which turn brown, deep orange, yellow, even gold before sundown. Watching the light change can be a way of living eternities within a day, of being free. I like knowing Beth watches the light too. Maybe we aren't so different.

In line to pay, we discuss a mutual friend who is pregnant, a son rising like bread beneath her shirt. She has a name picked out for him even though he's not due for another four months. We use the name fondly, like we've met him, and I start to feel love for it when I spot it out in the wild, like the baby is in me too. Like knitting or buying flowers, having a baby is aspirational, an optimistic reach toward the future. Am I capable of this? I want to be. Beth buys flowers like they'll be alive forever.

There's a guy at the deli who knows us from being regulars and offers us BLTs because that's what we order sometimes. His scruffy face is inviting behind the counter, eyes wrinkling near the tear ducts, his posture unceremonious. "The BLT girls!" he chuckles.

How sweet it is to be known. How sweet it is to carve routines into life.

My appetite returns, and I agree to the BLT. Tinfoil wrap swaddles the sandwich. I strip it off to reveal the crispy toast, cut into four triangles. A yellow burst of joy rushes up my spine. There is something so safe about this gesture, this cut. I soften and put my phantoms down. The deli guy mothers me. I have faith in the deli guy. Placing a five-dollar bill on his altar, I decide my belated New Year's Resolution will be to cut more sandwiches and have more sandwiches cut for me.

www.ingramcontent.com/pod-product-compliance
Lightning Source LLC
Chambersburg PA
CBHW071356160426
42811CB00112B/2290/J